CorelDraw How

The Fundamental of CorelDRAW

Steven Bright

INTRODUCTION

CorelDraw is a vector graphics design program. You can use CorelDraw to work with a variety of projects-from Invitation Card creation, Book cover design, Logo creation, Business card creation, Letterhead creation, Header/Cover image creation, Web graphics creation, Design Banner Ad, Design flyers, work with text and many other graphics design projects.

With this book, I bring to your aid my own personal CorelDraw manual. The various CorelDraw Tools and their uses are explained below to quickly get you on point.

PICK TOOL

Select the tool you want to use e.g. Polygon (star) from the "Tool bar". Hold down the left key and then move your cursor to the work space and click on it and the star will appear. You can now resize it.

UNPICK TOOL

To unpick a tool, click the "Pick Tool" tool (the first icon on the Tool bar).

MOVE OBJECT

To move an object, highlight the object and then place the cursor on its centre and a thick + sign will show. You can now hold down the left key and then move your cursor to the new location and release the left key.

SET OBJECT SIZE

To set an object size, go to the size feature on the properties bar and input the desired sizes (Width and Height) and then press the <Enter> key.

ROTATE OBJECT

To rotate an object, go to the size feature on the properties bar and input the desired angle, and then press the <Enter> key.

You can also double-click an object and then drag its rotatable handles to rotate it.

NUMBER OF SIDES

This is use to set the number of sides /points a polygon will have. Go to the number of sides/points feature on the properties bar and input the desired number, and then press the <Enter> key.

SHARPNESS OF AN OBJECT

Go to the number of sides/points feature on the properties bar and input the desired degree, and then <enter>.

CORELDRAW ENVIRONMENT

The main components of CorelDRAW Software Environment are:

- Work space
- Window
- Tool Bars
- Dockers and
- Pallets.

HOW TO USE THE BOOK

This is a documentation of know-how and not just knowledge. It entails an Introduction to CorelDraw Tools, Step by Step approach to working with these tools, Work flow, and Practical Graphics Design Projects.

To get the best from this book, you have to practice each and every step described in it. So, install CorelDraw and happily get to work.

.

CONTENTS

STEP BY STEP DESIGN PROCEDURES

PATTERN FILL

To fill a work with a pattern;

- Select the object.
- Click the Fill Tool from the Tool bar and then click the Pattern fill dialog box.
- Choose your option (2-color, Full color or Bitmap).
- Choose the patter of your choice from the scroll box.
- Set the Origin, Size and Transform properties as required.
- Click the OK button.

OUTLINE WIDTH

To change the Outline Width of an object, select it and then go to the number of sides/points feature on the properties bar and input the desired points and as you finish selecting the input, the effect will be created immediately.

You can also use the "Outline Tool" to perform this task. To do this;

- Select the object.
- Click on the "Outline Tool" from the Toolbar.
- From the Outline Tool dialog box, set the outline width. You can also set the object's Outline color or its line style.
- Click the OK button.

PUBLISH TO PDF

To publish a CorelDraw document to Portable Document Format (PDF);

- Go to File menu.
- Click "Publish To PDF".
- Click the "Settings" button to set the publishing custom specifications like its compatibility, export range, press quality, color management, compression type, and then click the OK button.
- Click the "Save" button.

EXPORT

To export a document, to PDF, JPEP or any other document format;

- Go to File menu.
- Click on Export.
- Type in the file name in the "File Name" field.
- Select file type from the "Save As" dialog box.
- Click the Export button.
- Set the bitmap properties from the dialog box (Image size, Resolution, Color mode, File size).
- Click the OK button.

REPEAT PATTEN

To repeat a pattern in one work on another work which are on the same work space;

- Select the work or objects.
- Go to "Edit" menu and click Repeat or CTRL+R and the object will be filled with the same pattern or color as the other.

PUBLISH FOR THE WEB

To prepare a CorelDraw file that will be published to the web, follow these steps;

- Go to File menu.
- Click on "Publish To The Web".
- Select the appropriate option (HTML, Web Image Optimizer).

- From the dialog box, set the publishing custom specifications like its export range, and HTML layout style in the case of HTML.
- Click the OK button.

WEB IMAGE OPTIMIZER

To optimize an image for web;

- Select the image or object.
- Go to File menu.
- Click "Publish To The Web.
- Select the appropriate option "Web Image Optimizer".
- Select file format.
- From the dialog box, type in the file name.
- Click the "Save" button.

PUBLISH FOR SERVICE BUREAU

To publish a document to service Bureau standard;

- Go to File menu.
- Click on "Publish To Service Bureau".
- Check the option button "Gather all files associated with the document" and click next.
- Check the option button "Copy font" and click next
- Check the option button "Generate PDF file" and click next.
- Chose the location to save the file and click next
- Click the "Finish" button.

Note: this help to produce and package the following: the CorelDraw (.cdr) document, a PDF of the document, job information, and Font information document.

RUNNING THE CALENDAR WIZARD

Calendar wizard comes with CorelDraw 11/12/13. To run the wizard;

- Go to Tools menu.
- Point to Visual Basics.
- Click "Play".
- From the dialog box, select "Calendar Wizard" from the drop-down list and then click Run.

PRODUCE CALENDAR

To produce a calendar using CorelDraw Wizard;

- Run the calendar wizard.
- Select the year from the "Year" drop down menu.
- Click the All button.
- Choose calendar language.
- Set the week start on.
- Click the "Holiday button" to set available holidays (Input the date and Name and then OK).
- Choose calendar layout from the "Layout" dialog box.
- Set the units (in, mm or pt).
- Set the margins.
- Click the generate button.
- Click the OK button.
- Click the Close button.

You can now perform further formatting or add images of your choice.

CORELDRAW MACRO

To save the steps used in creating a particular work, you have to create a macro while creating that graphic. The procedures to do this are:

- Go to Tools > Visual Basic.
- Click on record macro.
- You can now start your work (Note that all the steps you are using to create the work will be saved in the macro).
- Save the work when you are done.
- Go back to Tools>Visual Basic and click stop macro.
- To use a recorded macro, open a new document (CTRL+N).
- Go back to Tools>Visual Basic and click play macro.
- Click the OK button.
- The work will be recreated by the macro and this saves you a lot of time.

You can now use it as a template to create a related graphics design project.

TRANSPARENCY

With the transparency tool, you can make some objects transparent to show other objects.

To make a picture transparent so that a text written on it will be visible, do the following:

- Import the picture into the workspace and place it where it is required.
- From the "Tool bar" left-click on the drop down arrow on the "Interactive Blend Tool"
- Click on the "Interactive Transparency Tool"
- Click on the picture.
- Then left-click on one of the handles on the four corners and drag to the opposite corner.
- You can now pick the "Text tool" and any text written on this picture will be transparent (visible but not covering that part of the picture).

LAYOUT

With the help of layout, you can perform a high precision work. To use layout during your graphics design process;

- You can left-click on the vertical ruler and drag it on to you work.
- You can left-click on the horizontal ruler and drag it on to you work.
- You can use as many as both the vertical and horizontal rulers to guide you on what extend some objects should be placed.

FIT TEXT TO PATH

This is use to fit text to a predetermined path. To do this;

- Draw the shape that will provide the path (Ellipse, Sphere, Rectangle).
- Pick the Text tool.
- Take the cursor to the edge of the shape until a curve like line appears beneath the text symbol (A).
- At that instance, click the path and then start to type the text.
- Format the written text as required.
- Click on the path e.g. a circle until the outline box shows and then change its outline to none.
- Ensure that the text tool is still active, and then click on the object. From the task bar, you change the orientation of the text by clicking on the drop-down arrow and select the one of your choice.

FONT

To change the font of a text from the default font (Arial) to any other one;

- Select the text.
- Click on the Font drop down arrow and choose any other font of your choice and it will be automatically applied to it.

PEN OUTLINE

The pen outline dialog box is use to set the properties of an object. To do this,

- Draw the object e.g. a rectangle.
- Select the object.
- From the "Tool bar" left-click on the drop down arrow on the "Outline Tool".
- Click on "Outline Pen Dialog".
- From this dialog box, set the required properties such as (Color, Width, and Style).

- Click the OK button.

DUPLICATE AN OBJECT

To duplicate an object in CorelDraw;

- Select the object.
- Go to the "Edit menu" and click "Duplicate" or use CTRL+D.
- For multiple duplications, press CTRL+D as much of the duplicate you want.

You can now pick and make use of the duplicated objects in your graphics design project.

GROUP OBJECTS

To group objects in CorelDraw;

- Select the objects.
- Go to the "Arrange menu" and click "Group" or use CTRL+G.
- This will group all the selected objects into a composite object.

UNGROUP OBJECTS

To ungroup objects in CorelDraw;

- Select the objects.
- Go to the "Arrange menu" and click "Ungroup" or use CTRL+U.
- This will Ungroup the composite object to allow you access to its individual components.

GRAPH PAPER

To use the Graph paper Tool;

- Click on the "Graph paper Tool" from the Tool bar.
- Click on the insertion point on the document.
- From the property bar, locate the "Graph paper Column and Row size" and input the required number of column and row.
- Click anywhere in the document when you are done to insert the graph paper.
- Select the graph paper and click on the Outline tool.
- From the dialog box, set the color, and width properties to your choice.
- Click the OK button.

See the work below which has 2 columns and 21 rows.

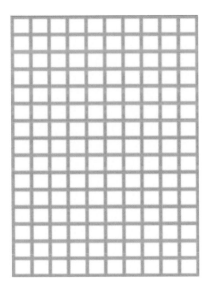

CREATE A 3D BOX

To create a 3D box;

- Pick the rectangle Tool and draw a rectangle.
- Select the rectangle and go to Effect>Extrude.
- From the extrude object manager dialog box, set the vertical points depth, height, and V.
- Click the Apply button.
- Select the 3D object and use the keys CTRL+K to break the shape.
- You can now apply colors to the front alone and another color to the other sides.
- Select the box and click on the outline tool where you can set the width to none.
- Click the OK button.

FOUNTAIN FILL

To apply fountain fill color to an object;

- Draw the object.
- Select the object.
- From the "Tool bar" left-click on the drop down arrow on the "Fill Tool".
- Click on "Fountain Fill Dialog".
- From this dialog box, set the required Color blend e.g from gold to orange.
- Click the OK button.
- Select the 0bject and change its outline width to none.
- Click the OK button.

BACK MINUS FRONT

To apply this to objects;

- Draw the two objects one on top of the other.
- Select all and center them by clicking the keys "C" and "E" respectively.
- Select the objects.
- Go to Arrange>Shaping (in the Property menu).
- Click "Back minus Front".
- Select the object and change its outline width to none.
- Click the OK button.

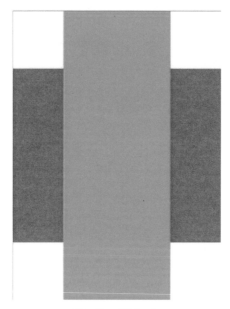

Starting Objects

Final object

FRONT MINUS BACK

To apply this to objects;

- Draw the two objects one on top of the other.
- Select all and center them by clicking the keys "C" and "E" respectively.
- Select the objects again.
- Go to Arrange>Shaping (in the Property menu)
- Click "Front minus Back".
- Select the 0bject and change its outline width to none.
- Click the OK button.

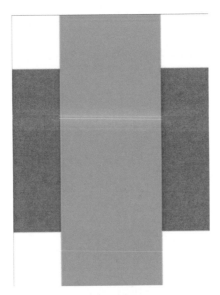

Starting Objects

Final object

WELD OBJECTS

To apply this to objects;

- Draw the two objects one on top of the other.
- Select all and center them by clicking the keys "C" and "E" respectively.
- Select the objects again.
- Go to Arrange>Shaping (in the Property menu)
- Click "Weld".
- Select the object and change its outline width to none.
- Click the OK button.

Starting Objects

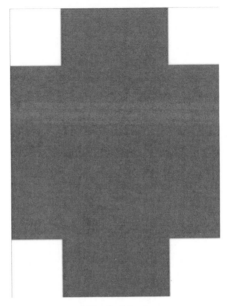

Final object

TRIM OBJECTS

To apply this to objects,;

- Draw the two objects one on top of the other.
- Select all and center them by clicking the keys "C" and "E" respectively.
- Select the objects again.
- Go to Arrange>Shaping (in the Property menu)
- Click "Trim".
- Select the object and change its outline width to none.
- Click the OK button.

Starting Objects

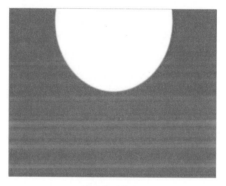

Final object

INTERSECT OBJECTS

To apply this to objects;

- Draw the two objects one on top of the other.
- Select all and center them by clicking the keys "C" and "E" respectively.
- Select the objects again.

- Go to Arrange>Shaping (in the Property menu).
- Click "Intersect".
- Select and delete the two original objects to unveil the result of the Intersect.
- You can now select the intersecting shape and apply the color of your choice to it.
- Select the object and change its outline width to none.
- Click the OK button.

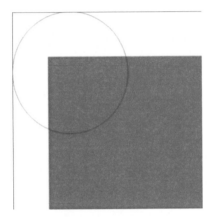

Starting Objects

Final object

COMBINE OBJECTS

To apply this to objects;

- Draw the two circles, a big one and a small one with one on top of the other.
- Select all and center them by clicking the keys "C" and "E" respectively.
- Select the objects again.
- Go to Arrange> (in the Property menu).
- Click "Combine".
- Select the object and change its outline width to none.
- Click the OK button.

See the works below, the first one is an object made up of a big circle and a small circle filled with two different colors. After combining them, they become a single object which now has only one color:

Starting Objects

Final Combine Result

SHAPE AN OBJECT

To shape an object you must first ensure the object is a curve e.g. a circle. If it is not a curve (rectangle, star, square), then you must first convert it to one.

- Draw the two objects one on top of the other.
- Select all and center them by clicking the keys "C" and "E" respectively.
- Select the objects again.
- Go to Arrange>Convert to curve or use CTRL+Q.
- Pick the "Shape Tool" from the tool bar and click on the object.
- Click drag on any of the frame ends to shape as required.
- Select the object and change its outline width to none.
- Click the OK button.

Starting Object

Final Shaping Tool Result

POWERCLIP

To use this tool;

- Draw the two separate objects.
- Select the object you want to clip onto the second one.
- Go to Effects>PowerClip.
- Click "place inside container".
- Click anywhere inside the bigger object.
- Should you want to extract out the second object, select the clipped object and then go to Effects>PowerClip>Extract.
- Select the object and change its outline width to none.
- Click the OK button.

Starting Objects

Final Powerclip Result

CONTOUR

To apply contour to an object and create either a center, inside or outside separate object;

- Draw the object.
- Select the object and go to Effects>Contour.
- From the contour dialog box, select either Center, Inside or Outside option.
- Input the contour Offset and Step values.
- Click the Apply button.
- Then press the keys CTRL+K to separate the created object from the original object so that it can be formatted separately.
- Select the object and change its outline width to none.
- Click the OK button.

Starting Object

Final Contour Result

WORKFLOW

Always create all your graphic components in a single document. Avoid the temptation of creating components in separate documents, thereby exporting some to .jpg format to re-use in some other works which can at times reduce their quality.

You can create a single work from various .cdr files by opening a new document, open the separate component documents and then copy them one after the other into the composite document and then combine them to form the single graphic.

COLOR MANAGEMENT TIPS

Even though color management in CorelDraw is a bit complex, the simple approach to it is to use CYMK (Cyan, Magenta, Yellow, and Black) colors if the work is intended for printing and RGB (Red, Green and Blue) colors will be ok if the work is only meant for on screen purposes.

STENCIL

To make a banner and print the work using Tiled pages with A4 paper instead of going to a printing press and then trace and dab onto the banner material. To do this;

- Set the size of the banner e.g. 3"*5".
- Write the text.
- Select all the text and click the crossed rectangle on the top of the color palette to remove the color.
- Select all the text and click on the Outline tool and then change the Outline width to 0.1"
- Click the Ok button.
- Use CTRL+P to bring up the print page and the click "Print preview".
- Click the "Print Tiled Pages" icon just to the left of the Inches and it will now be broken into several pages.
- Click the print icon to print it.
- Trace cut the printed A4 pages letters out.
- Get your banner material of the required size.

- Starting from the first page, place the stenciled texts on the banner and dab it with colors of your choice.
- You can now expose it to dry when you complete the work.

PUBLISH BOOK

The procedures for publishing your book with CorelDraw are stated below:

- Create a new page.
- Set up the page by going to Layout>Page Setup or simply double-click the page border and then choose twice the real size e.g. if the book size is 14*20cm, choose 28*20cm.
- Still from the Layout dialog box, go to "Layout" and then choose Booklet and also tick the "facing pages" box.
- You can now set text styles and the margins by allowing Guidelines.
- To get the last single page, click the plus sign, to reveal the next two pages e.g. 16-17 and then right-click on the page number 17 and click "Delete Page" to leave page 16 as the last single page number.
- Prior to printing the document, make sure the last single page is the one displayed on the screen to get proper document arrangement. Then got to

File>Publish to PDF. Input the document name, and choose Save as type and the PDF style as "PDF for Prepress". Still on the dialog box, go to settings and enter the "Author name" and then click publish to PDF button. You can now print from this PDF format..

Note: with the above setup, the first page and last pages will be single while the other pages will be in the other in which they will be read i.e. 2-3, 4-5, 6-7, 8-9, etc

LOGO DESIGN

To create and design a logo is like working on any other graphics design project. But it has some unique qualities since it serves a great purpose of being the face of an entity (company, organization, cultural groups, etc.).

There are therefore some important things you must put in perspective when working on a logo project as a graphics designer. Some of these things are:

- You must first have basic information about the organization or company that needs the logo.
- Conceptualize some samples.
- Create the logo.
- Use colors that depict the nature and operation of the entity.
- Send samples to your clients to get feedback from them.
- Use the feedback from the client to perfect the chosen design from the different samples sent to him/her.
- Send another sample again.

- Finalize the project using the last feedbacks.
- Export the logo as a PNG file.
- Get paid and then send the final design to your client.

To export a logo correctly such that the client can use it in his/her own design without the problem of whit background showing along with the logo, follow these steps:

- Use CTRR+E to bring up the export dialog box.
- Set the file type to PNG and input the file name.
- Set the output size as 300*300 pixel or per your clients requirement
- From the Export dialog box, check the option box on "Anti-aliasing", "Apply ICC profile" and "Transparency". Note that the first two are mostly checked by default. The most important point here is therefore to check the option box for transparency as this help to remove the white background.
- Click the OK button.
- From the next Export dialog box, check the option box on "Masked Area".
- Click the preview button to have a feel of how the background will be.
- Click the OK button.
- The logo has now been exported as a PNG file without a background, which is the standard practice in logo design.
- Note that the first sample contains four different types of logo which were exported together.
- To export a particular one of them, you will need to select that one and then check the option box

"Selected Only" from the export dialog box during the exporting processes.

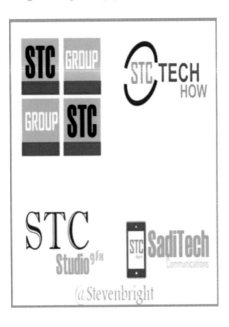

CALENDAR DESIGN

To design calendar in CorelDraw13, you will have to play the calendar wizard. To do this;

- Go to Tools and click Visual Basic.
- Click Play from the drop-down list.
- From the dialog box, select Calendar wizard from "Micros in" drop-down list.
- Click the run button.
- The calendar wizard is opened and you can now design the calendar by putting in the relevant and required details like year, week starts on, Holiday, Font to be use, etc.
- Select the Create calendar I current document to place the calendar in the currently opened document.
- Click the Generate button.
- From the finish dialog box, click OK.
- You can now reformat the calendar headings, add images, or any other custom details.

If you select all months, you now have a calendar of all the twelve months in 12 different pages which you can publish to PDF. You can also export each page as a .jpg graphic. See the one month calendar example below:

EBOOK COVER DESIGN

The two major components of a cover page are:

- The copy (content).
- The Artwork (image).

A book Cover requires brainstorming about it's make up as relates to the book content itself. There should be proper selection of themes, colors, and depiction of genre and fonts.

In the case of an eBook cover; some of the things to consider are:

- It size should be within the range 1600" * 2500" pixel.
- Keep the design simple and original.
- It should be clear even as a thumbnail.
- It must be good and professional because it is the first part a potential buyer have contact with and hence will determine the sales of the book.

- You have to be creative while designing an eBook cover.
- It should make sense and communicate the book genre to readers.

Below are examples of my eBook Cover design works.

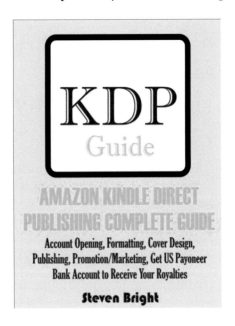

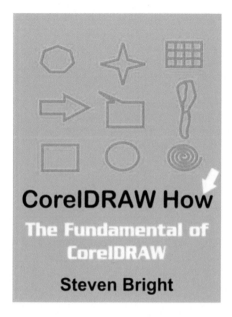

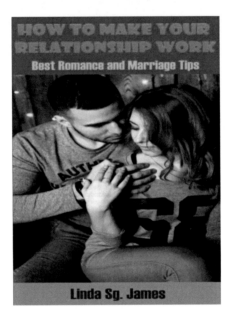

CD COVER DESIGN

The basic procedures for designing inside CD cover are as follows:

- The standard CD size is 12*12 cm.
- Draw a circle of 12*12 cm.
- Draw another circle of 2*2 cm inside the first one that will provide the required center hole.
- Select the two circles and go to Arrange>Click Trim.
- You can now applied the required color and create the required text on it.

COVER IMAGE/HEADER DESIGN

With CorelDRAW know-how, you can design a professional Header or Cover Image for your social media channels like Twitter, Facebook Page or Group, Google+ and many others. To do this effectively, you need to know the specific dimension for those graphics required by the various social media channels e.g. Twitter header image dimension is 1252px *626px (width by height).

Follow the steps below to design a professional Twitter header image.

- Draw a rectangle
- You should already know the choice of colors for your design.
- Fill the rectangle with colors.
- Write and arrange the texts on it as appropriate.
- Export the graphic using CTRL+E and from the Export dialog box set the unit as pixel and the size as 1252px*626px.
- Click the Export button.

- Your header image is now ready and can be uploaded to your Twitter account as the header image without experiencing any "image upload error message".

CONCLUSION

The above outlined graphics design steps and procedures are useful for any graphic work that is produced with the use of CorelDraw.

They were written out of practice and all the works or examples in this book are products of the application of these guides and tips.

SHORTCUTS

CorelDraw most important Shortcut keys are enumerated here and their uses stated.

SHORTCUT	FUNCTION
CTR+F12	Opens the spell checker, checks the spelling of the selected.
CTR+F10	Opens the Options dialog box.
Shift+F3	Opens the Change case dialog box.
CTR+Shift+PgDn	Selects text from the beginning to the end of frame.
CTR+Shift+PgUp	Selects text from the beginning to the end of line.
CTR+Home	Moves cursor to start of frame .
CTR+End	Move cursor to end of frame.

Shift+F12	Opens the Outline color dialog box.
F12	Opens the Outline Pen dialog box .
CTR+E	Export Objects to selected file format.
CTR+I	Import content into your document.
CTR+R	Repeat the last operation.
CTR+D	Duplicate the selected object.
CTR+G	Group the selected objects.
CTR+U	Ungroup the selected objects.
F9	Displays a full screen preview of the drawing.
Alt+F11	Lunches visual basics applications editor.
F1	Opens the help document.
CTR+K	To break 3D extruded box.
CTR+L	To combine objects.
PRESS "C" and "E"	To centre objects horizontally and vertically, select the objects and then press "C" and "E" respectively.
CTRL+Q	To convert selected object to curve.

ABOUT THE AUTHOR

Steven Bright is an Engineer, Tech expert, Graphics designer, Web developer, eBook formatter, and Blogger. He is also the Author of:

1. JavaScript Fundamentals: JavaScript Syntax, What JavaScript is Use for in Website Development, JavaScript Variable, Strings, Popup Boxes, JavaScript Objects, Function, and Event Handlers.

2. Amazon Kindle Direct Publishing Complete Guide: Account Opening, Formatting, Cover Design, Publishing, Promotion/Marketing, Get US Payoneer Bank Account to Receive Your Royalties.

3. Photoshop Beginner Guide: Photoshop Tools and their Functions, Photoshop Tools Practice, Color Management, File Formats, Photography, and Graphics Design.

4. Tools and Function Lists: Engineering Tools Manual.

5. Microsoft Word: Customizing the Quick Access Toolbar, Equations, Underline Styles, Insert Menu, Table, Page Layout, Formatting a Document, Edit Manuscript, and Preparation of an eBook for Publishing.

6. Microsoft Office Productivity Pack: Microsoft Excel, Microsoft Word, and Microsoft PowerPoint.

7. Computer Fundamentals: Introduction to Computer, Uses of Computer, Main Components of Computer, Input/Output Devices, Hardware/Software, Operating System, Internet, and More.

8. Microsoft PowerPoint: Creating a Presentation, Tips for Creating and Delivering an Effective Presentation, and Marketing Your Brand through PowerPoint Presentation.

9. Microsoft Excel: Microsoft Excel User Interface, Excel Basics, Function, Database, Financial Analysis, Matrix, Statistical Analysis.

10. Master Cascading Style Sheets (CSS) Quickly: CSS Properties, CSS Property Definitions, Inline CSS, Internal CSS, External CSS and Sample Codes.

11. The ABC of eBook Publishing: Kindle Direct Publishing, Draft2Digital, Smashwords, Writing, Formatting, Creating an Active Table of Content, and Marketing Guide.

12. Windows Operating System: Windows Operating System (OS) Installation, Basic Windows OS Operations, Disk Defragment, Disk Partitioning, Windows OS Upgrade, System Restore, and Disk Formatting.

13. Facebook Groups for Authors: How to Use Facebook Author and Book Promotion Groups to Generate Sales and Create Visibility for Your Books.